AF591378

Walk Of Shame

Jessica F'ing Exner

"I faced it all and I stood tall
And did it my way"
- Frank Sinatra

"Oh, I get by with a little help from my friends"
- The Beatles

"Looking like a true survivor, feeling like a little kid. I'm still standing after all this time"
- Elton John

2019 Jessica Exner. All rights reserved.
978-0-359-49046-2

www.facebook.com/jessica.fing.exner

Cover image by Anthony Haley
www.facebok.com/murmurmonsters

Edited by Alex Andrews

To the me that believed she was loved... You were never Fucking wrong.

To my sweet little children, Turtle and Rocket, I hope you are forever proud of your mother, the tears she shed and the strength she showed through them all.
I am forever grateful to be yours.

I wanted to do things a little bit differently this time around.

First and foremost, I wanted to do this process as much on my own as possible... I mean, I've asked for help, but, I am conscious to who, and for what.

This book, seriously, is more for me than anyone else. I needed to prove that I can, so that I can believe, with or without my last year's relationship, I would have made it here on my own anyways. I don't ever want to say I am who I am, or I have only accomplished these things because of someone else... And, I cannot confidently say that about the original publishing of my first collection "Flowers In The Margin" or even the second.

So much has happened in the relatively short time since its first printing, mostly heart ache and embarrassment but, I've also grown, a lot, and learned more about myself as a woman, lover, and mother.

Secondly, I also wanted this collection to be simpler. There is no rhyme or reason to the placement of pieces, they were literally all individually drawn from a hat and placed in the order the were chosen and I would like to think Carlee had something to do with the selection as I used her hat

Lastly, the title "Walk Of Shame" comes from the idea that I literally have NO reason to feel ashamed of the love I experienced and openly shared last year.
So, what? I made a fool of myself... but I also made lasting memories.
So, I had my heart ripped out of my fucking chest and sent through a meat grinder, but, I actually felt loved. I felt accepted and connected for the first time, ever. I was shown that even though it doesn't always work, there are partners and people who will cherish me and help me grow. People who don't go out of their way to make me feel little, or without power.
So, we aren't going to run off and get married, I won't carry his babies or go as his date to his cousin's wedding. But, I will live. I will love. I will be loved. And, I will be F'ING amazing as always. Even if I did tell him I want his dick to fall off the day before I wished him true happiness. That doesn't, in anyway, make either of them not true, nor does it make me any less of a badass boss. It just means that, for a moment, I let the red wine and anger become friends and take care of my feelings of abandonment for me.

So, here I am, walking away.. And there's no where to go but UP from here.

Table of Contents

*Trigger warning

Grieving Never Ends

If I could grant
Just one little wish for you,

It would be
For when you were alive

For you to
See yourself the way I do.

Maybe then
You could have survived.

Maybe then
You'd still be alive.

Dad Up

I wish that you were a better man.
Not for me, of course.

I don't know or understand
How you can not call with no remorse.

Lame-ass excuses,
And trust misuses,

You're a fucking idol dude-
A role model of sorts.

You need to "dad up."
Not for me of course.

Or you need to Fuck off.
Not for me, of course.

Acceptance

Today was friggin' great
But it was no fucking hope.
As soon as the sun went down
I couldn't even cope.

Who am I kidding?
The sky was still bright
When I cried your name
And now we're deep into night.

My crying turned to calling,
Burning our bridge and falling
Right into the ice-cold depths
Of bittersweet fucking regret.

Rainbows

I got stuck in the rainbow
You left behind.

I keep pieces of you
As a peaceful remind

That sooner or later
All will be fine,

And that then and now
You were always mine.

Mine to love,
And mine to have,

And for that
I am forever grateful.

Cum for Anyone

Thinking about
What it would be like

To be single again,
Getting dressed up and
Out for the night.

Drinks and boys and
Drinks and girls and

Dancing to the bands,
Swaying my hands
Like the world can't hold me back

And my options are endless
I could stay here till closing

Or I could go home with them
And we could lose our clothing.

Let them ravish me,
Take what needs to be taken.

Give 'em what they want
Even though I'm faking,

'Cause I don't cum
For just anyone.

But, I Don't Want To

I've got this perfect couch
Outside on the porch,

It's got a cozy slouch
And I could light a torch

If I wanted to.

I consider some nights
Sleeping out here

When the temperature is right,
When the sky is clear.

I could

If I wanted to.

Drift away to the sound of swaying trees
A bitter reminder that everything leaves

I could,

But, I don't want to.

Fight Your Fears

What are you afraid of?

Honestly,
Consider that for a minute.

Question yourself as long as you need to.

Figure it out
And when you do,

When you come to the conclusion of your fears

Face them.
Look them in the eye,

And then wreck them.
Please,
Beat them
Till they bleed through the streets.

Destroy every fucking glimpse there ever was

And move on

For you,
For me,
For us.

Don't Love Me

Whatever you do
Don't love me.

Don't waste your energy.
It won't last,

It never does.

What's going to happen
Is simple;

For a second
It's light and fun and airy,

And then
I'm everywhere.

Anywhere you look
You'll find parts of me.

Your dreams will become mine
And all of mine will be put aside,

And what you want
I will want.

And what you need
I will need.

From me
There is no free.

Because
I will absorb every inch
Of all you wish
And find a way to obtain it.

But, you will not remain mine.

And that is just fine.

So, whatever you do
Please don't love me.

I can't afford to waste
My own energy now.

Burden

Begging for attention
From someone with no intention

To free me,
To accept me,
To need me.

Even though I'm hurting
Maybe I'm the burden

To call,
To text,
To love.

Or maybe, just maybe
I've been made to believe

I'm too much,
I'm not enough,
I'm too tough.

When the truth is
Clear as day;

I am glorious,
I am distinct,
I should be celebrated.

Grandma Knows Best

My grandmother taught me that
"Hate" is the strongest worst in the
English dictionary
And can never be taken back.

So, I do not hate you,

I loathe and detest you.
I dislike you greatly.

I abhor, abominate, despise, and
execrate you.

I feel an aversion towards you, a
revulsion of sorts.

I feel hostile and repelled by, and
sometimes even revolted by you.

I regard you with disgust and am
unable to bear or stand you.
I find you intolerable.

I shudder and recoil,
Shrink, when your name is mentioned.
I disrelish you.

Because even when there's nothing
There's still something

And I fucking hate that.

Butty Slutty

If I acted more like a slut
And sent pictures of my butt

I would get more attention
From the boys.

But my ass is flat,
My tummy is not.

All I've got to give
Is emotional noise
And my undying affection

And that is awfully ugly.

To My Youngest Child

I babied you,
I know I did.

I know for sure
Because it took everything in me
Not to title this "To my Baby."

The youngest born
Out of two
To me,

And I knew you would be my last
After all I had lost
Before you.
My last had to be you.

I cherished every tear
Even though
They were mere minutes apart from
each other.
I gave in to every fear
holding you close so you felt safe.

And now you are four.
You started kindergarten in
September.

You still cry for what you want,
And I cherish it less and less,
Trying so hard to do be my best
And feeling overly defeated.

You're wild and free,
But, you still need me,
And I did that.

Young Love

Nothing feels as good

As when I was young

Spending my days in mismatched socks,

Having way too much fun.

Playing Barbies in the basement

Back before the days of this disease

Created by a lifelong resentment,

Searching for some sort of release.

Playing Catch-Up

I dreamt of you last night
Like I usually do.
Nothing fancy really,

Just showing my dream world to you,
This life I've created
And visit every night.

It was nice to show you around
Since in real life nothing is right.

So, we walked, and I explained
As we toured around my make believe

But as it always does
We faced a bitter end.
You had to leave;
You always have to leave.

Fight Me

I fucking dare you,

But not with your hands,
Of course.
I'd never stand a chance.

And if you choose to use
A word or two,
Prepared for me to yell and cry at you.

Because confrontation frightens me
But I've stopped not saying my peace.

So, prepare my friends
For all conversations to have an
Emotional end,

'Cause I refuse to convince myself
What I feel isn't real,
And yet I refuse to stay quiet
About the real I feel.

Best Friend

You're not ever coming back.

Shooting stars and birthday candles
Can never change that.

You're the only theme
I beat around the bushes.

No savage emotion

'Cause I'm afraid to face
The place
Where you're not.

I'm ignoring reality,
Closing my eyes
Not ready to see,
Not ready to be

Angry.

With so much love it hurts,
Jessica F'ing Exner

In September

Do you remember
The last conversation we had?

I do.

It was over the phone
But that hasn't stopped me
From picturing you
On the other side of it.

Sitting out in the September sun,
Worried for a friend.

I imagine branches blowing behind
you
As you sat on a bench outside the
hospital,

Alone

With me on the phone.

For far too long after you were gone
I called you
just to listen to your voicemail.

I never want to forget what you sound
like;

What the voice of a goddess sounds
like.

What comfort sounds like.

I like to say
I live with no regrets.
I like to say
I face things and forget.
But I have one wish
I can never fill.
I have one dream
I want to come true
That never will.

If only we spoke longer that day,
If only I had told you
How much I really loved you.

Even though
I know you know,
And you knew I knew,
How much of it
Came from you.

Fake-Ass Friends

I'm not interested
In your fake idea of friendship.

How could I be your friend?
I am in love with you.

The fact you think
I will just comfortably become
One of those girls who shows up in
your inbox-

The ones you give just enough to keep
them holding on
Just enough to make them think you
might be inclined
To spending some time
one on one.

I'm so angry

I'm considering moving away,
Taking myself out of this town
And far away from you and
All the friends who knew
I loved you,
Because I can't stand the shame
Of loving the unlovable.

I thought it would be forever
And you let me believe it could be forever-
All the chances I gave you to walk away
Consequence free.

You refused
saying you weren't going anywhere
Yet here we are
Saying goodbye.

Void

It's been way too long since
I've heard you speak.
I'm not counting
But it's been 37 weeks

And your voicemail does no justice
the hundreds of times I've called,

The long nights
The lonely afternoons

And gloomy mornings too.
I just wish one time
I'd actually get through to you.

If you could log in
To your social accounts
You'd see notifications
Of ungodly amounts,

Cause I've loved every comment
I've come across displayed with your
name,
And every single picture or post

I've done the same.
It's all I've got,
Crazy or not,
To fill this void in me.

80 Baby

I wanted to be yours
For the rest of my godforsaken life.
I wanted to maybe make it to 80
Reading in a chair in the sun,
I'd take a break
And look up to find you snoring,
Sleeping the afternoon away.
And when I'd be 50
We'd have had a big party
And I'd have drunk way too much,
And you'd be pissed cause
I left all the cans
Upside-down in the sink
"To dry."
I wanted you to remind me
On my 67th birthday
That I'd always be older than you
And I would laugh..
And put cake in your face
And when I was 31..
I wanted to know for sure
That you were mine
For all of time
But, you left
You happily walked away
From everything that could have been.

Lost Control

In the beginning
There was only
An overwhelming aura of sadness.

Should have locked me away in
Arkham Asylum with that savage
madness.

Times are changing with the seasons
And this dejection turns to bitter anger

As the hours and days and weeks pass.
Your plea for my forgiveness is in
danger.

Not that you'll even ask.

Above Mentioned Three

I've never wanted much, really

Just a little love
Some little 'mes'
And a little land to call my own.

Not much, really,
Just the above mentioned three.

First;
A person,
A grown person who believes I'm kind
of Special

Even after they see my cry
About things no one ever cries about-
Like that song on the radio
That makes the hairs on my legs stand
tall

Or the tears I'll shed for
My first sprout this spring.

And not just thinks I'm special
But wants to be special too, in the eyes
of me.

See, I want that lame-ass kind of love
that
Last longer than the first fight.

Secondly;
I already have the little creatures I
created
And I am not disappointed
In any single way.

They bring me pride and power
Like nothing ever before
But, that's a love story for another day.

Thirdly;
Some land, I s'pose
Is a true want and need for me.

I want to live the rest of my days in a
little
Family home made perfect for me,
And the above mentioned three.
A place to grow.

And when I'm gone,
When I leave this earth
I want that home to be a place of
comfort
For the above mentioned three.

Really
Not much, at all . .

Dear Heart

Can you fuck off with all this shit
'Cause the thing of it is

I've always believed that love
Was a brain-made emotion -

Just like faith
Respect and
Devotion.

So, someone explain
Why it hurts so bad
Just to fucking breathe.

Sincerely,

A Swollen and Stressed Out Gut

Dirty Ex-Lover

(A Pretty Pervy Poem)

Dear Ex-Lover,

Is it so bad I want you
Under my covers?

Just you and me
And some Netflix maybe,

Those writers' hands
I've written about
Wrapped tightly around my throat.

Take away my breath
And the same with my dress,

'Cause you always have been
And always will be
Better than the rest.

I am officially obsessed
And it can't be tamed.

Not a single thing
Will take away

The internal ache
That's calling your name,
Other than

Those writers' hands I've written about
Wrapped tightly around my throat.

Doormat

At the foot of the walkway
From inside to out,
Allowing entrance
And a surface to wipe away
All the places you've stepped today.

Dirty and stained,
Frayed edges,
Faded phrase proving the days
It was still brand new.

But now,

Used up and worn out,
Absorbing the world you've ignored
All the traces of all the places
You've been before here.

Its exterior is coarse
And everything left behind
Has built a shell of remorse-

And when you leave
The doormat stays.
Rain helps it grieve
And remember the days

That it was still brand new.

Hurt People

I will not write about this
In hopes to cope.
I will not express myself
In hopes to cope.

Because hurt people hurt people.

You hurt me like she hurt you.
I will not take this hurt with me.

Because hurt people hurt people,

And I don't want to hurt people.

Morning Mantra

I wake up each morning
And repeat the following aloud:

"I have to be powerful!
I have to be powerful!
I HAVE TO BE POWERFUL!"
Because even when
I don't want to be powerful

I have to be.
I have to show these little beans
That sadness comes
And sadness goes
But, power,
True power comes
From the grace you carry
When you want to bury your face away
When the world is heavy.

Power is the light you shine
In the darkest of days.

Broken Children

To all the broken children,

I hope you find your glue,
The courage to begin,
And all the pieces you need too
To build a
Happy,
Healthy,
Brave
You.
Because no matter what any one has
said,
You deserve it.

Yours truly,
A Mended Adult

Beg Me, Baby

I refuse to beg for love,
But I will fight you.

When you say its not me it's you
It's not you,
It's us.

That's it.

You can say all the things
You want to say
About not being ready,

But I'm not leaving
And neither are you -

Because me and you
Are you and me.

All your broken pieces
Are mixed up in mine
And we're gonna build 'em back up-

Because putting them back together
Is how you fix busted things.

Gushiest BullShit

I just keep telling myself
This sadness will pass
But I don't know when.
How long does it last?

'Cause

Bedtime brings lonely tears,
5am I'm awake with dread.
Mornings hold the day's fears,
No smell of you left in my bed

And

Late night dinners
Make me consider
What you might be eating,
And with who.

So

Nothing seems to take away
This empty pit that's bound to stay
Right there in my gut,
'Cause I believe in me and you.

If It Ain't Broke

Those few little words
That powerful woman once said,
"If it doesn't fit, it isn't the perfect
dress."
Back before I had a crown on my
head
Will help this wounded heart get some
rest.

You were just a beautiful garment
Neatly hung in a window,
Perfectly placed to be found

By someone other than me.

Christmas Wish List

With Christmas coming

We made a list
Of all the gifts and to who.

Her little list began with me
And ended with you.

So, I asked what and how
"Flowers to her grave."

So, I explained

"There is no grave for us to visit
But you see this tattoo, she's right there in it."

I got hugs and kisses
And exclaims how she misses you

And I,
Now and always

Miss you too.

Friend

I thought you sent me a sign.

He shared with me
His life with you,
And I was hooked

Because I needed you,
I needed you so bad.

I latched on to the next best thing
And I believed he was it.

He was my new you

And when he left
I broke.

Was I wrong?
Was he not from you?
Was I not paying enough attention?

But, he was

And what I know now
Is that he was a path
A path to a better me.

I gained the ability to

Be a better, more open writer-

To express the smothering sorrow
Freely

In the arms of someone
Who truly cared.

And now, to the world
Built by the courage he provided.

So, thank you my sweet friend,
I am forever grateful
For the comfort you sent
Through the arms of a caring man.

Feed Me

I'm not sorry for being so needy.
I've got every right to be this greedy.

I'm deserving of all that I ask
And, the past is in the past.

I'm not sorry for being so greedy.
I've got every right to be this needy.

I deserve more.
I deserve better.

I deserve to be loved and accepted.

I deserve comfort and compassion.

And I'm gonna give it to myself,
'Cause

I'm not sorry for being this greedy.
I've got every right to be so needy.

Virtue

I've been patiently waiting
For you to come to your senses

But, in the meantime
You've been building fences.

So, now it's my turn

To make a choice
To mute my voice.

No more missed calls
At least not from me,

And I'm praying one day
You'll finally see

You're worth it.

Cry About It

I hope you're having fun,
Whatever it is you're doing.

I'm sitting in,
Overthinking,
Wondering,
And stewing.

All the times you ever lied
Are running through my mind,

And all I want is to rest my eyes.
They're sore and tired from
The tears I've cried.

Dear Mother

You are not
Allowed

To be angry
At the life

I have created
In your absence,

But you are invited
And encouraged

To join in.

Love, Daughter

Just Keep Grieving

They say the day will come
when I don't miss you as much.
I don't believe it.

People tell me all the time
That it will get easier.
I don't believe it.

Because today, on the anniversary of
your birth
I'm reminded
I cannot call and hear your voice,

And the anniversary of your death
Is just hours away
And I don't even have a choice.

The tears are falling.

The tears are falling.

Do you hear me calling

For you?

Good Morning Love

5am depression
She's here with a vengeance
To teach you a lesson.

You were sound asleep,
She's not concerned.
The truth she tells runs deep.

She haunts your sweet dreams
Where you're happy and warm,
Now you're wide awake
You're cold and mean.

But she's not concerned.

She's here to teach you a lesson

And you'd better be listening.

Dearest Bri

When people say how beautiful you
are
Their words seem unconvincing and
flat.
They must not be looking too far
'Cause babe, you're so much more
than that.

If the sun and moon had one single
home
It would be your stunning face,
And if the oceans and skies took on
one name
For you and it would be called the
same.

As calm as the flowing rivers and the
valleys deep
Are those personal standards and
morals you keep.

If I could I'd grow a garden of you
I'd nurture and love it through and
through,
Just so I could say I have something
As beautiful as you.

Alone

I think I'm doing alright.
I mean,
I don't leave my house some days

But, I've left the confines of my bed
And I've left tears on those pillows,
All three,
And the stuffed friends I've recently
collected.

I share my bed most nights now
With him,
Or the kids -
I can't stand to sleep alone.
So, the stuffed creatures stay
When they can't,
When it's dark
And I can't cope
With being alone.

I have food and things delivered to my
home
Because I don't want to be surrounded
By people sometimes.
Sometimes I want to be alone,

But not totally alone.
Just the kind of alone where there're
no questions asked.

Where no one is wondering what I
want in my coffee,
No one asking cash or debit,
Or if I'd like to sign up for their
fucking points card.

But also, the kind of alone
Where I can be heard if I want to be-
Kind of,
Like talking out loud to myself
And there's no one there to judge me.

They're all at the department store
Buying way too many things
They don't actually need,
Trying to fill the void
Of being alone.

Anne of Green Gables

Based on the pictures I've seen
She's desperately attractive,

And even though you set boundaries
I see now, you've retracted.

I wonder
Have you made it back to her bed?

I'm curious
Is she any good at giving head?

Does she give you all
you'll ever need?

Do you cuddle her

Or

Roll over to sleep?

Goodbye Sweet Lover

Did you ever think a time would come
When you would leave someone
feeling
The way she left you?

Cheated and unloved,
Heartbroken and abused?

But, I know
You know
Better than anyone

The monster you've become,

The diminished soul you carry around

Where the torture originates from-

And that where you're looking is not
Where contentment is found.

Chatter Box

I have been so very patient
But it is starting to wear thin.

I'd like to bring it up
But where do I even begin?

And is it even, really, worth it
To discuss it, yet again?

Will I ever get an answer,
Or
End up crying to my friends?

Weak

He likes it when I'm strong
And he loves me when I'm weak.

As in he's the kind of guy
To give me wings when I want to fly,

And the one who holds me close
When I feel I need it the most.

Driver's Education

You took your power trip
Out for a rip,

Coasting the city limits
Between Refined, Unkind,
And a little place
I like to call Hell.

No regard for the people you're
passing
Or the piss warm rain splashing
From beneath your wheels,

The backlash of your fumes
Or how it actually feels
To be left

On the side of the road.

Grown-Ass Woman

I wanted to write about
How much better I am
Than all those other girls;

The ones who filled
Up all your time,
The girls who left us all
Reading between the lines.

I read again some of your jotted words,
Hoping to come up with a cute rhyme
And I was left unsure
Of what I got myself into.

Where do I even fit in?
Our hips don't sit
Perfectly entwined while we sleep.
It's far too sweaty in your shit-box
apartment
But I stay anyways,
3 fans and all.

And we don't spend our nights
Drinking or dancing,
Out in the bar,
Not thinking and
Stealing glances.

And we've never fucked in a bathroom stall-

Sure, I've got some kids
But the share the same dad
And he doesn't sleep on my couch,
And none of my other Exes do.
And none of my Exes have face tattoos,

And
I've got no knuckle tattoos,
But I have been known
To wonder where you are.
Like
"He texts me at 4:45 that he's on his way.
Do I have time to shower?
Maybe he will make a stop and I'll even have time to shave-
Ouu, and give a few minutes later in bed"

I've never Cut out a heart,
But I've cleaned up
The mess of mine
After it's been shredded
And destroyed
A time or two.

So, I've got some techniques
Tucked neatly up my sleeve
If you're interested in
Some heartache relief.

In conclusion, I'll never be that lady
I'll never love you the way she did,
But I'm not supposed to be
Because that little bitch was just a kid

And I'm a grown-ass Woman
With a dragon Heart,
The perfect protector of

Magic Items.

Fine and Dandy

"I didn't get your text"
Is all fine and dandy,

But it means you didn't think to check
And that's just fine and dandy

For someone you refuse to respect
Since your phone is always handy.

Tuna

When everything starts to fall around
you,
The pieces I could have helped you
pick up,
Remember me.

The late nights you can't sleep
through,
The coffee vs. tea battles we could
have endured,
Remember me.

When you're sad and lonely
And craving mustard with your tuna,
Remember me.

After a late night with a new friend
And she wants to stay the night,
Remember me.

When she begs you to love her
with all that you have
You'd better remember the me
That would have loved you better.

You'd better
Remember me.

She Loves Ya, Bud

If she says she loves you
She means it
With every speck of her insides,

Because words don't come to easy
But, feelings come way to fast-

And if she's said it out loud

It's 'cause she believed it would last.

She probably loves it when you fall asleep
Instead of the promises you try to keep,

And I know she loves how hard you work
To make your dreams come true.

Which means, she believes
That behind those lies
And beautiful blue eyes
Is a man that loves her too.

She clearly loves you just the way you
are

Because
It's seems no matter how hard you
push
She never gets too far,

Because she believes

In you.

She truly believes that behind those
lies
And beautiful blue eyes
Is a man that loves her too.

Huntsman

The thing of it is
I'll never recover.

I just keeping waiting
For you to come back.

Sadness and suffering,
While death takes another.

Connection Lost

Everything around me
Is dying.
If I were to say it didn't hurt
I'd be lying.

Maybe, I should stop making
connections
So, I don't suffer their loss,

Although it seems the simplest
It really is a selfish cost.

For, we were made to make
connections,
And we were made to face the
reflections
Of our choices,
Of our movements,
And how we use our voices.

So, I'm not ready to not know,
Not ready to not feel,
To not grow.

I'm not ready to not connect.

Bad Life Control

The pull-out method;

The one where I hold back,
Let my nerves take over.

"Everything's fine Jess,
Just go with the flow."

I can't...

What if...

No...

"It's alright babe,
Just let go."

I want to,

I really do.

Especially with you
But, I can't bear the consequences.

Not right now.
It's not the right time
And you know as well as I do
It's all about timing.

Last minute consider

We should have protected ourselves
A bit better,

But its far too late,
We're in too deep.

So, I'm pulling out now

Without a trace,

And nothing to reap.

Unobtainable

I'm so mad
I am mad that
I'm not good enough.
That you're willing to abandon
What we've created.
You promised you weren't going
anywhere.
You led me to believe you could love
me,
That you wanted to.
And now,
Now
I'm begging for you back
Like a starving dog.
What is so wrong with me
That all love is taken away
Or abused?
How could I allow myself
To believe in such a love
A love that doesn't even exist?
Because love,
Love is a compromise,
And I am an unacceptable
compromise.
There's no meeting me halfway.
I have to much
And there ain't a soul alive that could
reach
Even half my potential for love.
Why do I choose the unchooseable,
The unobtainable.

Why am I unobtainable?
A Mother's Promise

As your Mother
I promise to never

Speak negatively about the other
Adult in this endeavour.

'Cause even when you're thirty
You won't deserve the hurting

That comes from
Me
Being unloved.

But, I'm Feeling

I am feeling

Shaken,
Busted,
And ashamed.

The worst thing is
I'm the only one to blame.

But, I'm feeling

So, I know
I could have done better.

And, I know
I should have done better,

But, I also know
I am going to do better.

Space and Time

I wish I could go back in time
All the way to two thousand and five.

I'd fall in love with you again
And this time I'd do it better.

Not to say I want to be with you now,
I'm utterly and disgustingly happy for
you.

You just deserved better than the me
I gave you then.

I was toxic.
I was incredibly toxic.

Now, on a daily basis
I think of how better I am because of
you .

But when you think of me,
I know it's not nearly as neat and tidy,
or content.

It's messy
And, most likely, filled with regret,

And, sorry doesn't cut it.

I said it.

You heard it.

And, you even said it back.

But "Sorry" doesn't take away that
pain.
It doesn't make it all just go away.

It's there in you forever
Like it's here in me the same.

Broken Heart

I'm not exactly to sure how to say this
And, I definitely could never voice it
to your face,

But it breaks my heart
Every single day wondering

Why you can't love me.

And, the fact that you could
Just walk away tomorrow

Leaving me with out the slightest idea
To what I'd have done to deserve it-

I'm torturing myself,
Wanting so badly
To be accepted by you
Unconditionally.

Every part of us is there
Except you.

Flowers in the Margin

You got yourself a new notebook,
Somewhere to start a fresh story,

But in no time at all
All you could find

Were pages marked with my heart;

Annoying little flowers
In all your new margins

Written with pen
With no chance to be erased.

You wrote around them the best you could
But they were too distracting.

Your new story was never finished.

Your new notebook found a new home
On your shelf collecting dust

With all your other unfinished pieces.

Rough House

It's been a rough few days,
Bloody and bruised fingers.

Muscles so tight
I can barely stand.

She shows her face
In so many ways,

Wonder how long
She plans to linger.

She's mean and fierce
And she's back at it again.

FaceTime

I feel like what you're looking for
Is my number on a face
But when I consider my options
A number just isn't the case.

See I'm the time of day
When everything feels right
But I can't be specific
'Cause I'm also part of the night.

Sometimes I represent
When the sun is setting or, rising
But, everyday is different
So, I have a hard time deciding.

All I can surely say is
I'm proud to face each day
As if it's my last
And that, they go by way too fast.

Regret

Could you smell the vulnerability
From where you started out,
The place we sent you
When we could no longer cope?

Could you taste the strength
From the cave you made
Out of lies and fear
and your curdled tears?

Are you finished yet?
Are you fucking done?
Just face your mistakes
And the regret,

Please,

Before death visits again
And one of us is gone.

Public Humiliation

When I drink
I'm a sassy little minx.
I've said and done things I'd like to forget
And, I've shared words I will always regret.

But, how could I refrain
From feeling you're to blame
Especially with the way
You slandered my name?

Unprofessional,
Disappointing,
And pitiful.
I believe you should feel ashamed.

What could I have truly done to deserve such treatment?
It's not my fault you let me believe we were in agreement.
I'm not accountable for your neglect.
I think it's time you self-reflect-

If you even know how.

I'll be here
When you're ready to apologize
Like I have done to you

A hundred undeserving times.

Love Note

Hey there babe
Could you write me a note?

Nothing too intense
Just a little anecdote

About where you want to go
'Cause, babe, I need to know,

What do you want from me?

And what's the future that you see

For yourself?

Hairy Fear

I haven't shaved my legs
In longer than ever before
And it's for the man upstairs.

The one who tells me
Every time he sees me
That he likes shorts season

And the shape of my legs.

I hope today
He feels sick to his stomach.

I hope the lengthy black hair
Haunts his day

The way his words
Haunt mine.

Cole

It happened again
And just like that
Another soul stolen
In seconds flat.

My wish for you
My sweet, sweet girl
Is that you find your peace
In that other world,

And, that we somehow find comfort
Here, where we have been left.
That the two of you have each other
And that you're both finally at rest,

Together.

Time Travel

If I could I'd go back
To when
I asked you to kiss me

Instead

I'd sit back
And
I'd beg you to leave.

If I could only retract
Then
I could set myself free.

Picture This

I have this picture of us on my desk.
Well, I did

It's gone missing now,
It was taken by my youngest kid.

The one who misses you more than I
do
And they've hidden it in their room.

So, I let them keep it there.
Taking it away seems unfair.

Maybe, I'll hang it up on their wall,
One more attempt to make their pain
small,

'Cause they're too little
For such a big sad.

But between you and me
It seems
I'm the only one who feels bad.

Release

It's all officially over
And I don't know how to feel.

I've been waiting almost a year
And I can't believe it's real.

Goodbye fight,
Goodbye fear.

Hello future,
I'm glad you're here.

Rainy Day

Rain, rain
Come and stay
Take this hurt
And wash it away.

Rain, rain
Please, stay
Soak my soul
And grow this heart today.

Let the lightning
Clear my thoughts.
Let this thunder
Take me to bed.

Even though I feel
Like dancing in it
I figure tonight it just
Won't be the same.

Tonight before you fall asleep
Will you say my name?

Love Poem

I share my love for things as easily as I
breathe.
I say I love something everyday.
Just a thing I notice I do.

So, it makes perfect sense to me
That you seem hesitant when I say
That I am in love you.

'Cause, I love that guy on the radio,
and I love that song we just heard,
And I love my friend who sings with
me
In the sense that I feel good in that
moment.

I love the moon in every phase.
I love the way the sky changes as the
sun lowers too,
and I truly love the earth and what it
can bloom.
They bring out feelings of joy that lay
dormant.

But you, my sweet love,
You piss me off
'Cause this is a totally
different kind of love-

A deep down in my gut

Internal comfort..
A peace of mind
Kind of love.
Meet Me Halfway

To catch a fish

Do you hold your worm
Above the water?

Do you dangle your hook
A foot above the brisk edge?

Do you force the fish to leave
Its place of survival?

Or

Do you release your reel

Let your bait feel the impact of the
unknown seas?

Allow your hook to hit the depths your
buoy provides?

The fish makes the choice
To be hooked,
To be taken.

Don't dangle your heart
Over another creatures' ocean,
Teasing with false intentions.

Teeter-totter

Back and forth
But we're still here
Again, for you to
Clear up your fear.

You left behind
Your heart for sale
So, there's no point
To this useless fight.

You and me,
We're the same,

Only different.

Unblocked

It has been an uncomfortable amount
of time
since I last sat at my computer desk to
write.

It's riddled with kids toys,
Pictures to be hung,
And miscellaneous junk just waiting
for a home.

I want so badly for things to keep
moving
But I just keep moving things from
one place to another.

Maybe one day I'll quit bitching.
Maybe one day my kids will stop
fighting every word I speak.
Maybe, one day, I'll feel alright from
morning till bed.
Maybe one day I'll find a love that
doesn't leave.
Maybe one day I'll quit bitching.

Old Friend

Carlee,

I am in need of your friendship now,
more than ever.
I am in need of your acceptance now,
more than ever.
I am need of your honesty now, more
than ever,

Not the kind of biased truth
that comes from someone else's view.

I am in need of you now, you make
me better.
I am in need of your words now, you
make me better.
I am in need of your love now, you
make me better.

The kind of love that enraptures every
part of me
that comes from your unstoppable
belief in me.

Talks of Suicide

I'm honestly not suicidal
But I have honestly wondered
If leaping from my balcony would kill
me
Or just leave me badly hurt.

I'm not really suicidal
Though, I've really considered if my
children are better off with me around,
all sad and uncooperative,
Or if that's just a thing they say to make
you wanna stay.

I'm not actually suicidal
'Cause in all actuality I love my life;
I love being a mother, and a friend,
and a woman.

But that doesn't stop the gnawing voice
that's giving me the choice
And explaining it's not worth the
constant fuss of the morning rush
Or the fight to fall asleep at night.

Seriously, I'm not suicidal
But, I am seriously exhausted.

Quick Question

How would you feel if
You never heard from me again?

Like

If all you ever got
Were glimpses from a distance
And stories from our friends?

If I didn't answer your calls or texts
Would you be left with regrets?

Or would you be getting a better
night's sleep
Knowing that you're free from me?

TIA

Social Media

I made the mistake
Of searching your name

And read
Your most recent thread.

Now, here I am crying
Wishing you could feel the same,

Just wishing I had
The power to make you live this
dread.

This constant ache,
This inconsolable sadness,

But I can't.

And I guess that shows
How much more I care
About us than you.

You are fucking toxic.

Coward

Let's pretend we're just friends, ya?

That's what you want

To get together a time or two

Where I don't fight and cry for you.

Text me every now and then

Like I haven't been begging and

Explaining

Why none of this makes sense,

But it's never going to happen.

Cause you walked right in and made yourself comfortable.

You let me believe we were something worth talking about

And, I clearly still do.

Look at me up here wasting my breath,

Still talking about you.

Self-Checkout

What's the issue?

There are 10+ cash registers
all staffed with one or two,

And now there's a place to go
For all the people just like me

When speaking aloud ain't easy
And we're covered in anxiety.

And there's staff there too
If we decide we need some help.

So, there's not much an issue
For those who check out ourselves.

The Idea of Me

"You don't love me, you love the idea
of me"
Nah, bitch.
The idea of you keeps me up at night,
Tossing and turning
And terrified.

The idea of you has me questioning
everything:

My life,
Where it is,
Where it's going.

Your life,
Where it is,
Where it's going,

What they've ever been.

The idea of you has me ready to run-
Ready to drop all we've done together
And fucking book it
And not ever look back.

The idea of you is nauseating.
It rots my dreams while I sleep.
My once pretty-happy place
Is dark and dingy and lonely.

But then there's you
The real living breathing you
and when we're in the same room.

I am calm,

I am content,

I am still,

I am well.

Thank You

I wish I could mimic
The sound of rain,

The gentle drips
That tap the treetops,

And the pounding drops
That drown the drains

As the roaring thunder
That brings me to my knees.

I'm tucked away
In my little spot,

Praying to the Universe
And, thankful for the life I've got.

Satisfied

Honestly
I don't even know what I am doing
anymore.

I feel sad most of the time;
Sad and heavy.

My emotional weight is
Getting to be more than
I'm comfortable carrying around
Everywhere I go.

But, what am I even to do about it
Cry.
I could cry.
I have cried.
I think I'm bored of crying
Or maybe I've run out of tears.

Just add it to the list of things
I no longer feel like doing:

Dishes
Laundry
Crafting
And Crying
Etc, Etc...

And why?

'Cause I let someone in.
'Cause I exploited my vulnerability for
a few likes
And a couple more followers.

And, now
Now I'm forced to accept it,
To discuss it,
To bask in it,
To make a fucking story of it.
Something worth sharing of course.

Give the people what they want
Or they'll show up in your inbox
Asking questions that are none of their
fucking business.

Satisfied?

Carlee

One year ago today
I stood in front of one of
The strongest women I've ever known.

She sat there and told me her daughter
had died.
I fell.

I don't know how long it took to start
breathing again
Or, until I finally broke sound and
cried.

A mother lost her child
And yet she held my head on her
knee,

Wiping my tears and doing what she
could
To reassure me
That we would get through this.

She collected from inside
A bookmark made by me
"To auntie Car-car,"

One of the few possessions with her
when they found her body.

She told me,
She told me she'd always have us with
her.

And I didn't believe her,
I didn't.

I said I did, but I didn't
But she did.

She carried us everywhere she went-
She loved us.

She loved me
Fully and completely.

Summer Lovin'

I've been dreading summer
'Cause after summer it will be
September,

And in September
I'll be forced to remember

How badly it hurt
When you were taken

From me.

Thoughts And Prayers

Pray if you want to.
Share your story with the sky.

Tell it all about your troubles,
How the world is changing and needs help.
Pray your fucking heart out

But, children are still being taken from their families,
Placed alone in shelters,
And told their parents are criminals
For wanting a better life.

And homeless neighbours are still starving,

And teens are still being shot in their schools,

And there is so much suffering in our world

And in our communities.

But, pray your fucking heart out

'Cause clearly someone's listening,

Just not to you.

My Favourite Month

If I get a call one morning
And am told I should be mourning
'Cause your life had been taken
By the choices you're making,

I will mourn you
But more than that,

I will hate you.
I will be angry with you.
I will hate that you have left me.
I will be angry you're not around to
take my calls-

But in reality

You're already not around to take my
calls.
You have already left me here alone,

Wondering where you are,
Wondering how you are,
Wondering
Where you are.

The End

It seems as though
you've made your choice.

You said your piece
without a voice.

And I'm left again
Fearing for the end,

Begging for some kind of closure
Just trying to get some sleep.

Kept up all night replaying shit in my head,
Rehearing the promises you said you'd keep.

But, I am ready, ready to leave you here,
Ready to face the risks and take that leap.

I am ready
For The End.

So here I am, walking away. It feels more like floating now, though, not like in the beginning. When I stared this journey, I felt shattered and heavy. Like a bag of dampening concrete... just thicker and thicker with every tear drop. So, I set all the work aside and was NOT ready to face all the ache, and fucking bullshit that was left in the wake of what I thought was a forever kind of love. But then, I realized I am still the Powerful Beauty Queen Goddess I always believed I was, and just because one person couldn't see it is not a reason to stop counting the people that can. I opened up the files, I finished the unfinished pieces, and I created another project that I am incredibly proud of. And this time I did it in my own way, with friends, and contacts I am grateful to have. And there is so much power in that, I recently shared some of this struggle with a new friend, and as I explained where I started and who I was in the end, I could feel the pride pouring from my pores. I was Glowing, I could literally feel it. So, I am proud As Fuck, and incredibly grateful and astonished by the team of amazing spirits I have come to love and appreciate.

One specific little angel I would like to mention again. For anyone who read "Flowers In The Margin" you will know this beautiful grace, Alex Andrews. She has been inspiring me since before I knew her name. With a force flowing through her, she is constantly thriving to be a better version of herself, and encouraging those around her to do the same. There is absolutely nothing more empowering than that. She took some time from her very busy life to sit with me and listen, and take note, of all the things I wanted from "Walk Of Shame" judgement free, in my messy home. And through tears of pride and joy and anxiety, I shared all of my hopes and dreams for this project and she did her part to make them a reality. And she did it with a smile and a kind heart. I am forever grateful for her and her love for grammar.

Another familiar name, one I hope to mention in all of my future projects, Anthony Haley. He created yet another astonishing cover. He took all of my mismatched emotions, needs and wants and portraying them better than I could have ever imagined. There are really no words to express how thankful I am for this beautiful rendition of a lifelong journey that has lead me to this point in my life, a position in which I can say, I am truly proud.

And finally THANK YOU so much for taking the time to read through these lame emotions, I hope you smile knowing I am smiling, BIG. And, if I can read through the saddest shit I wrote while the sadness was still raw and fresh, YOU CAN DO ANYTHING.

Thank you,
And also, you're F'ing
WELCOME.

www.ingramcontent.com/pod-product-compliance
Ingram Content Group UK Ltd.
Pitfield, Milton Keynes, MK11 3LW, UK
UKHW020221250726
13967UKWH00001B/118
9 780359 490462